AF581244

You Are Capable Of Amazing Things!

You Are Capable Of Amazing Things!

You Are Capable Of Amazing Things!

You Are Capable Of Amazing Things!

You Are Capable Of Amazing Things!

You Are Capable Of Amazing Things!

You Are Capable Of Amazing Things!

You Are Capable Of Amazing Things!

You Are Capable Of Amazing Things!

You Are Capable Of Amazing Things!

You Are Capable Of Amazing Things!

You Are Capable Of Amazing Things!

You Are Capable Of Amazing Things!

You Are Capable Of Amazing Things!

You Are Capable Of Amazing Things!

You Are Capable Of Amazing Things!

You Are Capable Of Amazing Things!

You Are Capable Of Amazing Things!

You Are Capable Of Amazing Things!

You Are Capable Of Amazing Things!

You Are Capable Of Amazing Things!

You Are Capable Of Amazing Things!

You Are Capable Of Amazing Things!

You Are Capable Of Amazing Things!

You Are Capable Of Amazing Things!

You Are Capable Of Amazing Things!

You Are Capable Of Amazing Things!

You Are Capable Of Amazing Things!

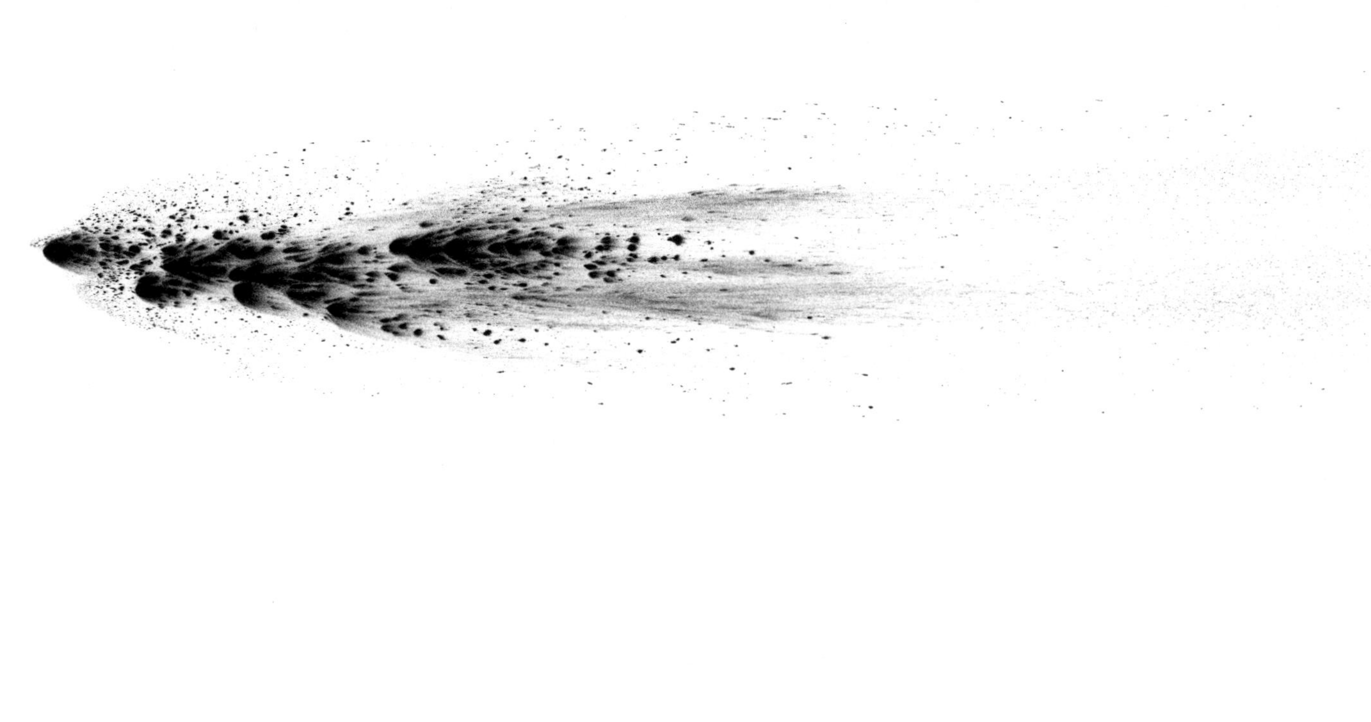

You Are Capable Of Amazing Things!

You Are Capable Of Amazing Things!

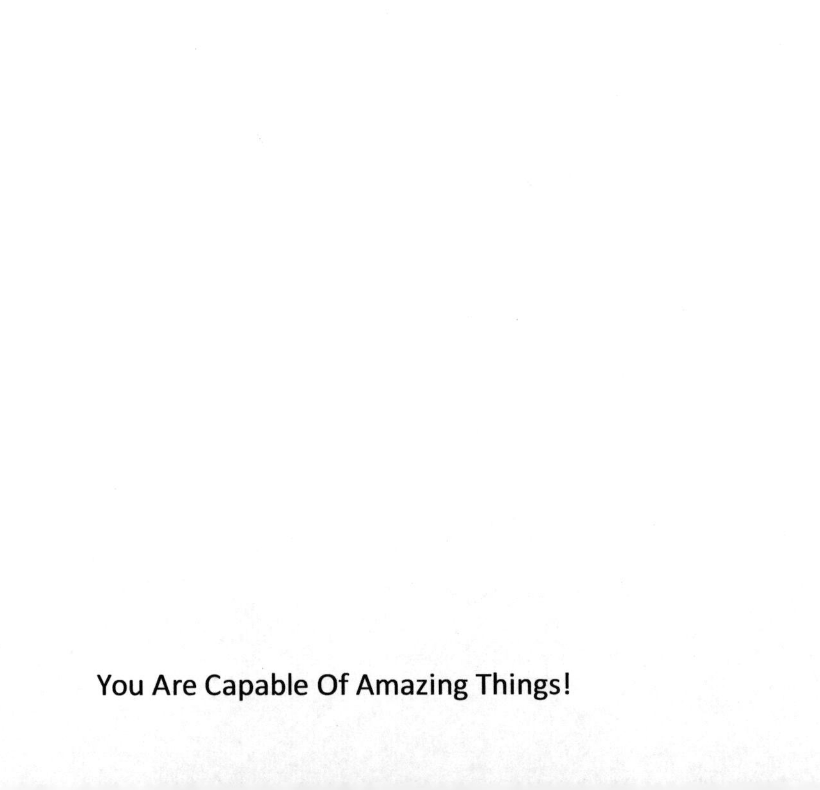

You Are Capable Of Amazing Things!

You Are Capable Of Amazing Things!

You Are Capable Of Amazing Things!

You Are Capable Of Amazing Things!

You Are Capable Of Amazing Things!

You Are Capable Of Amazing Things!

You Are Capable Of Amazing Things!

You Are Capable Of Amazing Things!

You Are Capable Of Amazing Things!

You Are Capable Of Amazing Things!

You Are Capable Of Amazing Things!

You Are Capable Of Amazing Things!

You Are Capable Of Amazing Things!

You Are Capable Of Amazing Things!

You Are Capable Of Amazing Things!

You Are Capable Of Amazing Things!

You Are Capable Of Amazing Things!

You Are Capable Of Amazing Things!

You Are Capable Of Amazing Things!

You Are Capable Of Amazing Things!

You Are Capable Of Amazing Things!

You Are Capable Of Amazing Things!

You Are Capable Of Amazing Things!

You Are Capable Of Amazing Things!

Made in the USA
Las Vegas, NV
29 November 2024